Alto Saxophone

Level 2–3

Alfred's
INSTRUMENTAL
mp3
CD
PLAY-ALONG

Ultimate
Christmas
Instrumental Solos

MW00999479

Arranged by Bill Galliford, Ethan Neuburg, and Tod Edmondson
Recordings produced by Dan Warner, Doug Emery, Lee Levin, and Artemis Music Limited.

© 2013 Alfred Music
All Rights Reserved. Printed in USA.

ISBN-10: 0-7390-9911-6
ISBN-13: 978-0-7390-9911-7

Alfred

 Alfred Cares. Contents printed on 100% recycled paper.

CONTENTS

A HOLLY JOLLY CHRISTMAS

Track 2: Demo
Track 3: Play-Along

Words and Music by
JOHNNY MARKS

Track 4: Demo
Track 5: Play-Along

ANGELS MEDLEY
(Angels from the Realms of Glory/Angels We Have Heard on High)

Angels from the Realms of Glory
Words by JAMES MONTGOMERY
Music by HENRY SMART

Angels We Have Heard on High
TRADITIONAL

BELIEVE
(from *The Polar Express*)

Track 6: Demo
Track 7: Play-Along

Words and Music by
ALAN SILVESTRI and
GLEN BALLARD

Moderately slow (♩ = 80)

BLUE CHRISTMAS

Words and Music by
BILL HAYES and JAY JOHNSON

FOLK CAROL SUITE
I. Noël Nouvelet

TRADITIONAL FRENCH CAROL

Track 10: Demo
Track 14: Play-Along

Folk Carol Suite - 5 - 1

Track 11: Demo
Track 15: Play-Along

II. Masters In This Hall

TRADITIONAL FRENCH CAROL
Words by WILLIAM MORRIS

Folk Carol Suite - 5 - 2

III. Coventry Carol
(Lullay, Thou Little Tiny Child)

Track 12: Demo
Track 16: Play-Along

TRADITIONAL ENGLISH CAROL

Track 13: Demo
Track 17: Play-Along

IV. O Du Fröhliche/Echo Carol

By J.D. FALK and
HEINRICH HOLZSCHUHER

CAROL MEDLEY
(Hark! The Herald Angels Sing/O Come, All Ye Faithful/The First Noel)

Track 18: Demo
Track 19: Play-Along

Carol Medley - 2 - 1

13

Carol Medley - 2 - 2

CELEBRATION MEDLEY
(Hallelujah Chorus/Joy to the World)

Track 20: Demo
Track 21: Play-Along

Majestically (♩ = 88)
Hallelujah Chorus
By G.F. HANDEL

Joy to the World
By G.F. HANDEL

Celebration Medley - 2 - 1

DO THEY KNOW IT'S CHRISTMAS?

(Feed the World)

Track 22: Demo
Track 23: Play-Along

Words and Music by
BOB GELDOF and MIDGE URE

Do They Know It's Christmas? - 2 - 1

FELIZ NAVIDAD

Track 24: Demo
Track 25: Play-Along

Words and Music by
JOSÉ FELICIANO

Feliz Navidad - 2 - 1

FROSTY THE SNOWMAN

Track 26: Demo
Track 27: Play-Along

Words and Music by
STEVE NELSON and JACK ROLLINS

Bright swing (♩ = 168) (♫ = ♩³♪)

HAPPY XMAS
(War Is Over)

Words and Music by
JOHN LENNON and YOKO ONO

Track 28: Demo
Track 29: Play-Along

GESÙ BAMBINO

(The Infant Jesus)

Music and Italian Lyrics by
PIETRO A. YON

Gesù Bambino - 2 - 1

HAVE YOURSELF
A MERRY LITTLE CHRISTMAS

Track 32: Demo
Track 33: Play-Along

Words and Music by
HUGH MARTIN and RALPH BLANE

I'LL BE HOME FOR CHRISTMAS

Track 34: Demo
Track 35: Play-Along

Words by KIM GANNON
Music by WALTER KENT

26

INFANT HOLY, INFANT LOWLY

Track 36: Demo
Track 37: Play-Along

TRADITIONAL

JINGLE BELL ROCK

Track 38: Demo
Track 39: Play-Along

Words and Music by
JOE BEAL and JIM BOOTHE

IT'S THE MOST
WONDERFUL TIME OF THE YEAR

Track 40: Demo
Track 41: Play-Along

Words and Music by
EDDIE POLA and
GEORGE WYLE

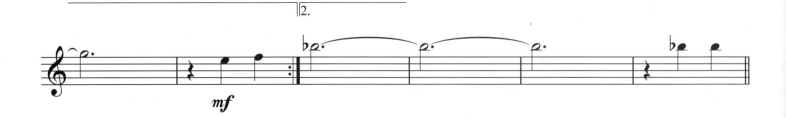

It's the Most Wonderful Time of the Year - 2 - 1

It's the Most Wonderful Time of the Year - 2 - 2

JINGLE BELLS

Words and Music by
JAMES PIERPONT

LET IT SNOW! LET IT SNOW! LET IT SNOW!

Track 44: Demo
Track 45: Play-Along

Words by SAMMY CAHN
Music by JULE STYNE

LO, HOW A ROSE E'ER BLOOMING

Track 46: Demo
Track 47: Play-Along

TRADITIONAL CAROL

MANGER MEDLEY
(Away in a Manger (Cradle Song)/Away in a Manger/Silent Night)

Track 48: Demo
Track 49: Play-Along

Moderately (♩ = 84)

Away in a Manger (Cradle Song)
TRADITIONAL CAROL

Away in a Manger
TRADITIONAL CAROL

Silent Night
TRADITIONAL CAROL

MARY, DID YOU KNOW?

Track 50: Demo
Track 51: Play-Along

Words and Music by
MARK LOWRY and
BUDDY GREENE

Slowly, with a half-time feel (♩ = 50 or ♩ = 100)

Mary, Did You Know? - 2 - 1

GROWN-UP CHRISTMAS LIST

Track 52: Demo
Track 53: Play-Along

Words and Music by
DAVID FOSTER and
LINDA THOMPSON JENNER

Grown-Up Christmas List - 2 - 1

Track 54: Demo
Track 55: Play-Along

O CHRISTMAS TREE
(O Tannenbaum)

TRADITIONAL CAROL

O HOLY NIGHT

Track 56: Demo
Track 57: Play-Along

TRADITIONAL CAROL

Slowly, with expression (♩. = 66)

ROCKIN' AROUND THE CHRISTMAS TREE

Track 58: Demo
Track 59: Play-Along

Words and Music by
JOHNNY MARKS

Moderately bright (♩ = 72) (♫ = ♩³♪)

Rockin' Around the Christmas Tree - 2 - 1

Rockin' Around the Christmas Tree - 2 - 2

RUDOLPH, THE RED-NOSED REINDEER

Track 60: Demo
Track 61: Play-Along

Words and Music by
JOHNNY MARKS

Moderately slow and expressive (♩ = 92)

SLEIGH RIDE

Track 62: Demo
Track 63: Play-Along

Composed by
LEROY ANDERSON

Moderately bright, with spirit (♩ = 100)

*A♯ = B♭, E♯ = F♮

SANTA CLAUS IS COMIN' TO TOWN

Track 64: Demo
Track 65: Play-Along

Words by
HAVEN GILLESPIE

Music by
J. FRED COOTS

Santa Claus Is Comin' to Town - 2 - 1

THE LITTLE DRUMMER BOY

Track 66: Demo
Track 67: Play-Along

Words and Music by
KATHERINE DAVIS, HENRY ONORATI
and HARRY SIMEONE

WE WISH YOU A MERRY CHRISTMAS

Track 68: Demo
Track 69: Play-Along

TRADITIONAL CAROL

UKRAINIAN BELL CAROL

Track 70: Demo
Track 71: Play-Along

TRADITIONAL CAROL

Moderately bright, in one (♩. = 56)

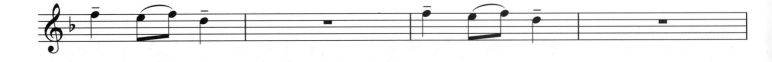

Ukrainian Bell Carol - 2 - 1

WINTER WONDERLAND

Words by
DICK SMITH

Music by
FELIX BERNARD

YOU'RE A MEAN ONE, MR. GRINCH

Track 74: Demo
Track 75: Play-Along

Lyrics by
DR. SEUSS

Music by
ALBERT HAGUE

Themes from
THE NUTCRACKER SUITE

Track 76: Demo
Track 81: Play-Along

Composed by
PETER ILYICH TCHAIKOVSKY

Themes From the Nutcracker Suite - 6 - 1

March

Brightly (♩ = 152)

53

Themes From the Nutcracker Suite - 6 - 2

Dance of the Sugar-Plum Fairy

Track 78: Demo
Track 83: Play-Along

Slowly (♩ = 56)

Russian Dance (Trepak)

*An easier alternative note has been provided.

**B♯ = C♮

56

Track 80: Demo
Track 85: Play-Along

Waltz of the Flowers

Bright waltz, in one (♩. = 60)

*B♯ – C

Themes From the Nutcracker Suite - 6 - 5

**E♯ = F♮

PARTS OF AN ALTO SAXOPHONE AND FINGERING CHART

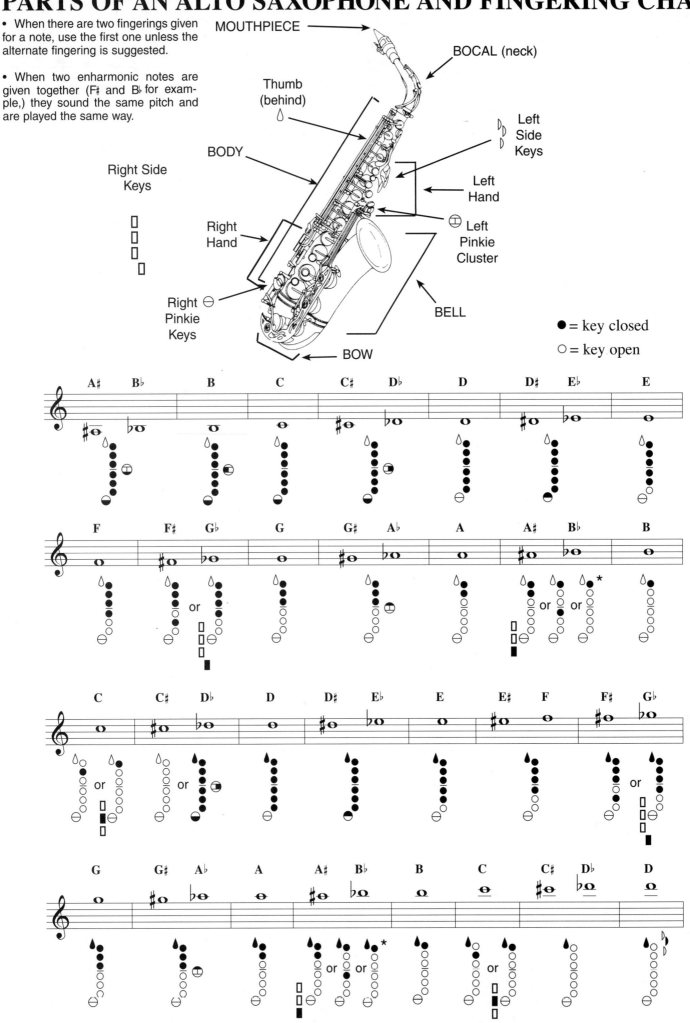

* Both pearl keys are pressed with the Left Hand 1st finger.

Alfred Music Is Your
Ultimate Resource for Play-Alongs

Alfred's Play-Alongs include a fully orchestrated play-along & performance demo MP3 CD, including Alfred's Tempo Changer Software and a PDF of the piano accompaniment.

The Hobbit: An Unexpected Journey Instrumental Solos

Music composed by Howard Shore
This beautifully produced folio features an array of colorful photos from the film. Titles: My Dear Frodo • Old Friends • Axe or Sword? • The Adventure Begins • Warg-scouts • A Good Omen • Song of the Lonely Mountain • Dreaming of Bag End • A Very Respectable Hobbit • Erebor • The Dwarf Lords. (Guitar book also available)

Ultimate Movie Instrumental Solos

Contains 60 songs, including: Cantina Band • Follow the Yellow Brick Road / We're Off to See the Wizard • Gollum's Song • Hedwig's Theme • James Bond Theme • Obliviate • Pink Panther Theme • Raiders March • Superman Theme • Wonka's Welcome Song • and many more.

Ultimate Pop & Rock Instrumental Solos

Includes 60 songs—great value! Titles: 21 Guns • 25 or 6 to 4 • A Whiter Shade of Pale • Animal • Blueberry Hill • Both Sides Now • Dancing Queen • Desperado • Domino • Don't Stop Believin' • Dynamite • Everybody Talks • Firework • and many, many more.

Easy Christmas Carols Instrumental Series

These compatible arrangements can be played together or as solos. Titles: Angels We Have Heard on High • Away in a Manger (Medley) • Come, Thou Long-Expected Jesus • Go, Tell It on the Mountain • We Three Kings • Hark! The Herald Angels Sing • It Came Upon a Midnight Clear • Joy to the World • O Come All Ye Faithful • O Come, O Come, Emmanuel • O Little Town of Bethlehem • Silent Night • The First Noel • What Child Is This.

Each series includes books for the following instruments: flute, clarinet, alto sax, tenor sax, trumpet, horn in F, trombone, violin, viola, & cello.

Love Play-Alongs?

There's an App for That!

Play titles from Alfred's most popular play-along books with our new app. Available for iOS, Mac, and PC.

- **Auto scrolling, easy-to-read notation**
- **Loop sections**
- **Adjust song tempo**
- **Isolate Instrument in the mix**
- **Record your performance**

PLAY-ALONG
Powered by **Jammit**

alfred.com/playjammit

Harry Potter
INSTRUMENTAL SOLOS

Play-along with the best-known themes from the Harry Potter film series! The compatible arrangements are carefully edited for the Level 2–3 player, and include an accompaniment CD which features a demo track and play-along track.

Titles: Double Trouble • Family Portrait • Farewell to Dobby • Fawkes the Phoenix • Fireworks • Harry in Winter • Harry's Wondrous World • Hedwig's Theme • Hogwarts' Hymn • Hogwarts' March • Leaving Hogwarts • Lily's Theme • Obliviate • Statues • A Window to the Past • Wizard Wheezes.

(00-39211) I Flute Book & CD I $12.99

(00-39214) I Clarinet Book & CD I $12.99

(00-39217) I Alto Sax Book & CD I $12.99

(00-39220) I Tenor Sax Book & CD I $12.99

(00-39223) I Trumpet Book & CD I $12.99

(00-39226) I Horn in F Book & CD I $12.99

(00-39229) I Trombone Book & CD I $12.99

(00-39232) I Piano Acc. Book & CD I $18.99

(00-39235) I Violin Book & CD I $18.99

(00-39238) I Viola Book & CD I $18.99

(00-39241) I Cello Book & CD I $18.99

Alto Saxophone   Level 2-3

SELECTIONS FROM THE
Alfred's INSTRUMENTAL PLAY-ALONG
Harry Potter
COMPLETE FILM SERIES
INSTRUMENTAL SOLOS